GOD'S REST AND THE CATCHING AWAY OF THE SAINT'S

W. S. Scott

ISBN 979-8-89345-455-0 (paperback)
ISBN 979-8-89345-456-7 (digital)

Christian Faith Publishing
832 Park Avenue
Meadville, PA 16335
www.christianfaithpublishing.com

Printed in the United States of America

INTRODUCTION

AS I WAS attending my local church's study on prophecy and the book of Revelation, the Holy Spirit told me something very specific about the language used in some of the texts. It is only with this understanding, and considering what seems obvious about this prophecy, that the *Rapture* is unlocked.

What the Holy Spirit shared with me is how the text we are going to be looking at is inclusive, involving more than just the people mentioned, and how that opens what is written about our being caught up, raptured to meet Jesus in the air.

I don't consider myself a prophet, but I do consider these texts to be true.

> "Surely the Lord GOD does nothing Unless He reveals His secret counsel To His servants the prophets." (Amos 3:7)

And there is this:

> "It is the glory of God to conceal a matter, But the glory of kings is to search out a matter." (Proverbs 25:2)

The graph below shows the three most common teachings about the Rapture (catching away) of those who are alive and remain.

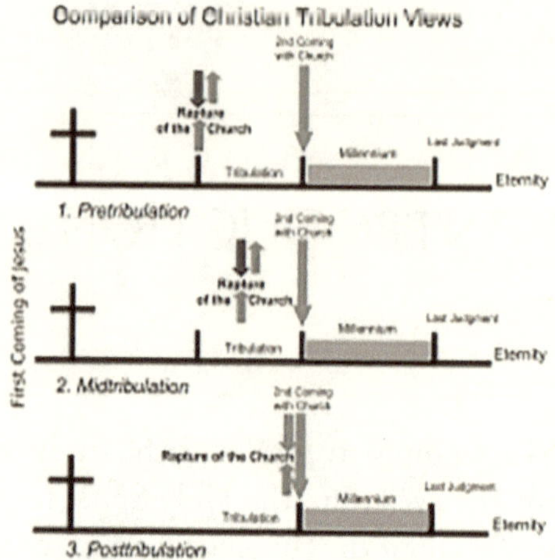

Rapture. (2023, July 27). In *Wikipedia.* https://en.wikipedia.org/wiki/Rapture

Among the many texts that let us know there will be a catching away of the church are these words of Jesus Christ Himself,

> "Do not let your heart be troubled; believe in God, believe also in Me. In My Father's house are many dwelling places; if it were not so, I would have told you; for I go to prepare a place for you. If I go to prepare a place for you, I will come again and receive you to Myself, that where I am, there you may be also." (John 14:1–3 NASB)

Before we take a look at the text, we need to consider some of the types of language or expressions used in the book. Most people who read the Bible are aware of things like poetry and metaphors. But in prophecy, there are telescoping events, beginning with the current events of the time of the prophet and then going well into the future. Inclusive and transference language involving more than one event or person.

While some people argue that the word *Rapture* does not appear in the Bible, it means to be snatched or suddenly caught up. It comes from the Greek word *harpazo* or, more directly, from the Latin *raptus.*

It is simply the word we use to describe the event in this text that is going to take place. Each of these views is based on assumptions. Let's take a brief look at each of these opinions and some of the problems each of them has.

PRE-TRIBULATION

THE PRE-TRIBULATION TEACHING is by far the most popular teaching in the United States. However, it is not as widely accepted in the rest of the world. It was first introduced in a writing referred to as "Apocalypse of Pseudo-Ephraem," attributing the writings to Ephraem the Syrian (AD 306–373). But many believe they were written much later by authors that Ephraem influenced. And there have been others through the years, but it became popular, primarily in the United States, through the teachings of Hal Lindsey, Jack Van Impe, and books like *Left Behind* by Tim LaHaye. Dr. Chuck Missler was also among these, and for me, he was also instrumental in helping me understand not to hold on to things I was taught too tightly.

"The only barrier to truth is the assumption you already have it." (Chuck Missler)

One of the main themes of this teaching is that Jesus will suddenly take the church to be with Him in heaven. And He will do so without warning, catching everyone by surprise, and setting the stage for the biblical prophecy of the tribulation period to begin. A second major theme of this teaching is that the Lord will bring with Him the dead in Christ and the church at His second coming. Meaning that the church must be caught up before this can take place and that the Rapture and the Second Coming are two separate events. This will prove to be true, but not in the way it is taught in these opinions.

"Now may our God and Father Himself and Jesus
our Lord direct our way to you; 12 and may the
Lord cause you to increase and abound in love for
one another, and for all people, just as we also do
for you; 13 so that He may establish your hearts
without blame in holiness before our God and
Father at the coming of our Lord Jesus with all
His saints." (1 Thessalonians 3:11 NASB)

This letter goes on to talk more about the resurrection of the
dead and our being caught up together with them.

"But we do not want you to be uninformed,
brethren, about those who are asleep, so that
you will not grieve as do the rest who have no
hope. For if we believe that Jesus died and rose
again, even so God will bring with Him those
who have fallen asleep in Jesus. For this we say
to you by the word of the Lord, that we who are
alive and remain until the coming of the Lord,
will not precede those who have fallen asleep. For
the Lord Himself will descend from heaven with
a shout, with the voice of the archangel and with
the trumpet of God, and the dead in Christ will
rise first. Then we who are alive and remain will
be caught up together with them in the clouds to
meet the Lord in the air, and so we shall always
be with the Lord. Therefore comfort one another
with these words." (1 Thessalonians 4:13–18)

We are also taught that Jesus will come before the tribulation
period begins without warning, like a thief in the night. But here in
chapter 5:4, we are told,

"But you, brethren, are not in darkness, that the
day would overtake you like a thief."

"Now as to the times and the epochs, brethren, you have no need of anything to be written to you. For you yourselves know full well that the day of the Lord will come just like a thief in the night. While they are saying, 'Peace and safety!' then destruction will come upon them suddenly like labor pains upon a woman with child, and they will not escape. But you, brethren, are not in darkness, that the day would overtake you like a thief; for you are all sons of light and sons of day. We are not of night nor of darkness; so then let us not sleep as others do, but let us be alert and sober. For those who sleep do their sleeping at night, and those who get drunk get drunk at night. But since we are of the day, let us be sober, having put on the breastplate of faith and love, and as a helmet, the hope of salvation. For God has not destined us for wrath, but for obtaining salvation through our Lord Jesus Christ, who died for us, so that whether we are awake or asleep, we will live together with Him. Therefore encourage one another and build up one another, just as you also are doing." (1 Thessalonians 5:1–11)

The pre-tribulation teaching suggests that this event will happen before the seven-year tribulation period begins and that the church must be taken out of the way because we are the ones holding back the man of sin, the Antichrist. I have never heard or read anything that supports this.

Some of the teachers holding to this understanding also believe that the entire seven years is the wrath of God, while others consider the first half to be the tribulation period and the second half to be the great tribulation and the wrath of God. They all believe that the church will be caught up before the tribulation begins because we are not appointed to wrath.

MID-TRIBULATION

T HE MID-TRIBULATION VIEWPOINT believes that the church will be raptured before the great tribulation begins, but we will go through the tribulation, which begins when the Antichrist negotiates a peace treaty with Israel and the Arab nations.

> "For God has not destined us for wrath, but for obtaining salvation through our Lord Jesus Christ, 10 who died for us, so that whether we are awake or asleep, we will live together with Him." (1 Thessalonians 5:9–10)

This view takes into consideration that in the book of Daniel, we are told that the saints will be given over to tribulation for "time, times, and half a time," or three and a half years.

> "He will speak out against the Most High and wear down the saints of the Highest One, and he will intend to make alterations in times and in law; and they will be given into his hand for a time, times, and half a time." (Daniel 7:25)

While I have not made an effort to study this viewpoint thoroughly, this understanding tends to hold a view that the Rapture will occur approximately forty-five days (about one and a half months) before the Antichrist stands in the holy place in the temple of God, when he will proclaim himself to be god.

I have not found anything to support or suggest that.

POST-TRIBULATION

I WAS FIRST INTRODUCED to the post-tribulation view in the mid to late 1990s by Irvin Baxter of Endtime Ministries, at a time when I had already begun to question and disagree with the pre-tribulation teachings I had been taught in Baptist and non-denominational churches.

One of the main arguments for this view is in the book of Revelation 12:12:

> "Now the salvation, and the power, and the kingdom of our God and the authority of His Christ have come, for the accuser of our brethren has been thrown down, he who accuses them before our God day and night. And they overcame him because of the blood of the Lamb and because of the word of their testimony, and they did not love their life even when faced with death. For this reason, rejoice, O heavens and you who dwell in them. Woe to the earth and the sea, because the devil has come down to you, having great wrath, knowing that he has only a short time."

The post-tribulation belief argues that "because the devil has come down to you, having great wrath," the wrath that occurs during the tribulation is the wrath of Satan and not from God. And that the wrath of God does not occur until the end of the tribulation at the battle of Armageddon, the hill of Megiddo.

The problem is that this view fails to consider chapter 11 where at the end of the first 1,260 days (about three and a half years) of the tribulation we are told:

> "And the twenty-four elders, who were seated on
> their thrones before God, fell on their faces
> and worshiped God, saying:
> 'We give thanks to you, Lord God Almighty,
> the One who is and who was,
> because you have taken your great power and
> have begun to reign.
> The nations were angry,
> and your wrath has come.
> The time has come for judging the dead,
> and for rewarding your servants the prophets
> and your people who revere your name,
> both great and small—
> and for destroying those who destroy the earth.'"
> (Revelation 11:16–18)

We see in verse 18, "The nations were angry because your wrath has come," God's wrath. In the last half of the tribulation, the great tribulation, the world will suffer the wrath of Satan and the wrath of God. The argument or belief about our return with Jesus is that after seven years of tribulation, God resurrects the dead, those that are alive are caught up, and that we immediately return with Christ. (Writing this out in a sentence warps my brain now.)

And so my effort so far is to briefly summarize the most common views of what is referred to as the Rapture. While the word *Rapture* describes the event, the catching away that will take place; it is something of a misnomer. God willing, what we will see is how the resurrection of the dead in Christ will happen first, followed by the catching away of the living to meet Christ in the air as prophesied in the text. We will be entering into God's rest when He lifts His hand of protection, the Holy Spirit, and the wrath of Satan is no longer encumbered.

LITERARY FORMS USED IN THE BIBLE

I F WE WANT to understand the Bible, it is important that we understand the context and types of language, or expressions, being used. One of my mentors said there are over two hundred types of language used in the text. I have not found any papers that describe all of these, but Bible.org has a paper on the subject titled "Literary Forms in the Bible" (bible.org/seriespage/iv-literary-forms-bible).

Most of us are familiar with poetry, prophecy, and parables, along with simile, metaphor, and personification, as used in Proverbs 8:2:

> "Does not wisdom cry out, and understanding
> lift up her voice?"

Another example of the language used in the Bible would be when animals and beasts are described. These symbols almost always represent countries, powers and principalities, or rulers and kings. An excellent example of this is Revelation 12.

In this chapter, the Bible describes a woman, which is Israel, with twelve stars on her head that represent the twelve tribes of the Jewish people, and a red dragon, possibly representing Red China and Satan, having seven heads, ten horns, and seven crowns on its heads. That's not the most common view, but it did not originate here or with me.

And then again in verses 7 through 9:

> "Then war broke out in heaven. Michael and his angels fought against the dragon, and the dragon and his angels fought back. But he was not strong enough, and they lost their place in heaven. The great dragon was hurled down—that ancient serpent called the devil, or Satan, who leads the whole world astray. He was hurled to the earth, and his angels with him."

We can see in these verses that the dragon is without question Satan.

Because these texts speak of "the male child," Revelation 12 is often taught as being about events that have happened in the past. When we consider the life of Jesus, that would be true. But when we look at all of chapter 12, we see that it points to things that are about to take place. Chapter 12 telescopes from the life of Jesus and His death and resurrection to halfway through the tribulation, the beginning of great tribulation, and the wrath of God and Satan's wrath also.

Prophecy often telescopes from the events that were happening when the prophet wrote the text to the future. It can also be inclusive, or transference, involving other people, times, or events.

WRONGLY TAUGHT

LET'S TAKE A look at some of the text that tells us the Rapture will take place. 1 Thessalonians is often quoted to support the understanding that the Rapture will take place suddenly and unannounced.

> "Now as to the times and the epochs, brethren, you have no need of anything to be written to you. For you yourselves know full well that the day of the Lord will come just like a thief in the night." (1 Thessalonians 5:1–2)

Virtually everyone who teaches that the church will be taken out of this world before the tribulation begins uses these two verses to support their argument. They may read all of chapter 5 but then only speak on verses 1 and 2. They can't see that this same paragraph tells us that we are not of the night.

If we read the entire paragraph the way it was written, it disqualifies that understanding.

> "Now as to the times and the epochs, brethren, you have no need of anything to be written to you. For you yourselves know full well that the day of the Lord will come just like a thief in the night. While they are saying, 'Peace and safety!' then destruction will come upon them suddenly like labor pains upon a woman with child, and they will not escape. But you, brethren, are not

in darkness, that the day would overtake you like a thief; for you are all sons of light and sons of day. We are not of night nor of darkness; so then let us not sleep as others do, but let us be alert and sober. For those who sleep do their sleeping at night, and those who get drunk get drunk at night. But since we are of the day, let us be sober, having put on the breastplate of faith and love, and as a helmet, the hope of salvation. For God has not destined us for wrath, but for obtaining salvation through our Lord Jesus Christ, who died for us, so that whether we are awake or asleep, we will live together with Him. Therefore encourage one another and build up one another, just as you also are doing." (1 Thessalonians 5:1–11)

The Apostle Paul goes on to tell us in verse 3:

"While they are saying, 'Peace and safety!' then destruction will come upon them suddenly."

That the people of this world, being in darkness, will be taken by surprise, like a thief in the night. Then he goes on to tell us:

4 But you, brethren, are not in darkness, that the day would overtake you like a thief; for you are all sons of light and sons of day. We are not of night nor of darkness; For God has not destined us for wrath, but for obtaining salvation through our Lord Jesus Christ, who died for us, so that whether we are awake or asleep, we will live together with Him."

Paul tells us that because we are children of light and are watching, we will not be caught by surprise.

"But you, brethren, are not in darkness, that the day would overtake you like a thief; for you are all sons of light and sons of day. We are not of night nor of darkness."

I know there will be a lot of people saying that just means we should be watching every day because we never know when He will show up like a thief in the night, and that is true because we never know what day our last day will be. That day when we will stand before Him. So we should always know that we could be in the presence of Jesus at any given time.

2 Thessalonians 22

"1 Now we request you, brethren, with regard to the coming of our Lord Jesus Christ and our gathering together to Him, that you not be quickly shaken from your composure or be disturbed either by a spirit or a message or a letter as if from us to the effect that the day of the Lord has come. Let no one in any way deceive you, for it will not come unless the apostasy comes first, and the man of lawlessness is revealed, the son of destruction, who opposes and exalts himself above every so-called god or object of worship, so that he takes his seat in the temple of God, displaying himself as being God. Do you not remember that while I was still with you, I was telling you these things? And you know what restrains him now, so that in his time he will be revealed. For the mystery of lawlessness is already at work; only he who now restrains will do so until he is taken out of the way. Then that lawless one will be revealed whom the Lord will slay with the breath of His mouth and bring to an end by the appearance of His coming; that is, the one whose coming is in accord with the activity of Satan, with all power and signs and false wonders, and with all the deception of wickedness for those who perish, because they did not receive the love of the truth so as to be saved. For this reason, God will send upon them a deluding influence so that they will believe what is false, in order that they all may be judged who did not believe the truth but took pleasure in wickedness." (2 Thessalonians 2:1–12)

In this letter to the church in Thessalonica, Paul is very specific:

(1) Make sure that no one deceives you by a false spirit, false prophet, or letter telling you Christ has returned. Or, moreover, for us, that we are in the millennial reign of Christ.
(2) That the day of the Lord will not come before the apostasy, the man of sin who is the Antichrist exalts himself to be god in the temple of God, the Jewish temple.
(3) Only he who now restrains will do so until he is taken out of the way.

People who teach the pre-tribulation view verses such as verse 7, "Only he who now restrains will do so until he is taken out of the way," as being the church, Born-again Christians. I do not know of anywhere in the text that refers to the church as being *he*, or masculine. The church is called the bride, or Christians are the bridesmaids. Or Israel being a woman or harlot.

The problem with the word *he* is that it is singular, pointing to an individual. For a long time now, I have considered that the one who restrains could be the Holy Spirit, but the problem with that is the word *he* is lowercase and does not point to God.

I expect to take another look at *who* this individual is and what is going to take place when he is taken out of the way. But for now, let's move on.

Mathew 24
And the Words of Jesus the Christ

Matthew 24 is often referred to as the Olivet Discourse or the Eschatological Discourse. It is a record of Jesus's response to the apostles when they asked Jesus about the signs of His return.

> "Jesus came out from the temple and was going away when His disciples came up to point out the temple buildings to Him. And He said to them, 'Do you not see all these things? Truly I say to you, not one stone here will be left upon another, which will not be torn down.'
>
> As He was sitting on the Mount of Olives, the disciples came to Him privately, saying, 'Tell us, when will these things happen, and what will be the sign of Your coming, and of the end of the age?'
>
> And Jesus answered and said to them, 'See to it that no one misleads you. For many will come in My name, saying, 'I am the Christ,' and will mislead many. You will be hearing of wars and rumors of wars. See that you are not frightened, for those things must take place, but that is not yet the end. For nation will rise against nation, and kingdom against kingdom, and in various places there will be famines and earthquakes. But all these things are merely the beginning of birth pangs.'" (Matthew 24:1–8)

Jesus begins answering the apostles by warning them, and us, that there will be many false prophets claiming to be the Christ, but are not. And that there will be wars, nation against nation, earthquakes, and famines. And that all these things must take place. But these things are not the end.

A lot of teachers today, and throughout the generations, try and point to these things as if they are getting worse and the end, especially the Rapture, is going to happen any minute. The truth is that these things have always been and always will be. Even if they have become somewhat worse, these things are birth pangs that must take place, but they are not the end. Do not let anyone deceive you as if they are anything different.

But then Jesus continues and says,

> "Then they will deliver you to tribulation, and will kill you, and you will be hated by all nations because of My name. At that time many will fall away and will betray one another and hate one another. Many false prophets will arise and will mislead many. Because lawlessness is increased, most people's love will grow cold. But the one who endures to the end, he will be saved. This gospel of the kingdom shall be preached in the whole world as a testimony to all the nations, and then the end will come.
>
> Therefore when you see the ABOMINATION OF DESOLATION which was spoken of through Daniel the prophet, standing in the holy place (let the reader understand), then those who are in Judea must flee to the mountains. Whoever is on the housetop must not go down to get the things out that are in his house. Whoever is in the field must not turn back to get his cloak. But woe to those who are pregnant and to those who are nursing babies in those days! But pray that your flight will not be in the winter, or on a Sabbath. For then there will be a great tribulation, such as has not occurred since the beginning of the world until now, nor ever will. Unless those days had been cut short, no life would have been saved; but for the sake of the

elect those days will be cut short. Then if anyone says to you, 'Behold, here is the Christ,' or 'There He is,' do not believe him. For false Christs and false prophets will arise and will show great signs and wonders, so as to mislead, if possible, even the elect. Behold, I have told you in advance. So if they say to you, 'Behold, He is in the wilderness,' do not go out, or, 'Behold, He is in the inner rooms,' do not believe them. For just as the lightning comes from the east and flashes even to the west, so will the coming of the Son of Man be. Wherever the corpse is, there the vultures will gather." (Matthew 24:9–28)

These words are prophetic. They are the words of Jesus pointing directly to Daniel's seventieth week, the seven years of the tribulation that was later prophesied in the book of Revelation by Jesus. He tells us that we will be hated by all nations. And that lawlessness will flourish, and that people's hearts will grow cold and uncaring.

Jesus then tells the apostles that we will be delivered into tribulation, and there will be a time of great tribulation. He also tells of a defining event, when the Antichrist will commit the *abomination of desolation*, proclaiming himself to be God. This must happen first.

What is remarkable here is verse 15 and the use of the word *Therefore*, meaning "for that reason," "consequently," or "as a result, so." And then in verse 20 is the word *flight*.

With the use of the word *therefore*, Jesus is telling us all that we will be delivered into this time of tribulation. But the word *flight* (in my opinion) is also telling us more than just telling the Jews to run for the hills.

And then the *Rapture*.

"But immediately after the tribulation of those days THE SUN WILL BE DARKENED, AND THE MOON WILL NOT GIVE ITS LIGHT, AND THE STARS WILL FALL from the sky, and the powers of the heavens will be shaken. And then the sign of the Son of Man will appear in the sky, and then all the tribes of the earth will mourn, and they will see the SON OF MAN COMING ON THE CLOUDS OF THE SKY with power and great glory. And He will send forth His angels with A GREAT TRUMPET AND THEY WILL GATHER TOGETHER. His elect from the four winds, from one end of the sky to the other." (Matthew 24:29–31)

After telling the apostles these things, He begins teaching in parables.

"Now learn the parable from the fig tree: when its branch has already become tender and puts forth its leaves, you know that summer is near; so you too, when you see all these things, recognize that He is near, right at the door. Truly I say to you, this generation will not pass away until all these things take place. Heaven and earth will pass away, but My words will not pass away. But of that day and hour no one knows, not even the angels of heaven, nor the Son, but the Father alone. For the coming of the Son of Man will be just like the days of Noah. For as in those days before the flood they were eating and drinking, marrying and giving in marriage, until the day that Noah entered the ark, and they did not understand until the flood came and took them all away; so will the coming of the Son of Man be. Then there will be two men in the field; one will be taken and one will be left. Two women will be grinding at the mill; one will be taken and one will be left." (Matthew 24:32–41)

It is here in these verses, 32 through 41, that we miss it. I don't know of anyone who sees all that God is telling us in these texts, texts that tell us of the days being like the days of Noah or the days of Lot.

And it is not without good reason that we don't understand and are mistaken about what will be going on at this appointed time. It is also in these same texts that we can gain a degree of insight into what will be taking place.

When a person is saved and first starts to study and learn from the Bible, we are taught that no one knows the day or the hour when Jesus will return, or when the Rapture will take place. And while that has been true, it makes it difficult to consider anything else.

This parable tells of two groups of people. But most of us only consider the second group, in the days of Noah, who were eating and drinking, marrying, and giving in marriage, until Noah entered the Ark. Those living in the world. Those not watching are caught unaware as by a thief in the night.

Most of us in the United States are taught that the church will be raptured and taken out of the world before Daniel's seventieth week even begins, in a pre-tribulation event. And at least most of those believing in a mid-tribulation event also believe that the church will be raptured before the abomination of desolation takes place. Even though both opinions point to certain scriptures to support their beliefs, they are based mainly on assumption.

But Jesus, in answering the apostles' question of what will be the signs of His coming, tells them in verse 33, "You too, when you see all these things," that we can know He is at the door. Those of us that are watching are more like Noah. And that we can know when we see the Antichrist do these things.

And to remind us, in 2 Thessalonians 2, verses 1 through 3, the Apostle Paul clarifies our being caught up:

> "With regard to the coming of our Lord Jesus
> Christ and our gathering together to Him, that
> you not be quickly shaken from your composure
> or be disturbed either by a spirit or a message or
> a letter as if from us, to the effect that the day

of the Lord has come. Let no one in any way
deceive you, for it will not come unless the apostasy comes first."

Let no one deceive you, because it will not happen unless…
The abomination of desolation by the Antichrist must take place first.
And to remind us of Paul writing in 1 Thessalonians 5:3,

"While they are saying, 'Peace and safety!' then
destruction will come upon them suddenly like
labor pains upon a woman with child, and they
will not escape."

They, the world, and those of us living in the world being worldly, will be taken by surprise. As by a thief in the night.

4 "But you, brethren, are not in darkness, that
the day would overtake you like a thief; 5 for you
are all sons of light and sons of day. We are not of
night nor of darkness." (1 Thessalonians 5:4–5)

But you, those that are alert and watching, those more like Noah, we can know as Noah knew.

But then a Warning
And Call to Repentance

After telling us that one will be taken and another will be left, Jesus gives us a warning.

Therefore be on the alert, for you do not know
which day your Lord is coming. But be sure of
this, if the head of the house had known at what
time of the night the thief was coming, he would
have been on the alert and would not have allowed

his house to be broken into. For this reason, you also must be ready; for the Son of Man is coming at an hour when you do not think He will.

Who then is the faithful and sensible slave whom his master put in charge of his household to give them their food at the proper time? Blessed is that slave whom his master finds so doing when he comes. Truly I say to you that he will put him in charge of all his possessions. But if that evil slave says in his heart, 'My master is not coming for a long time,' and begins to beat his fellow slaves and eat and drink with drunkards; the master of that slave will come on a day when he does not expect him and at an hour which he does not know, and will cut him in pieces and assign him a place with the hypocrites; in that place there will be weeping and gnashing of teeth." (Matthew 24:42–51)

These verses are part of why we have so much confusion about the church being taken out of the world because Jesus tells us to be on the alert because we do not know the day or the hour of His coming.

We are taught and understand this warning to be for everyone. But we fail to see what Jesus has said earlier. That no one knows, not the angels of heaven or the Son of Man knows the day or hour, but the Father alone. He also told us in response to our being gathered together with them in the air in the 15th and 16th verses:

"Therefore when you see the ABOMINATION OF DESOLATION which was spoken of through Daniel the prophet, standing in the holy place (let the reader understand), then those who are in Judea must flee to the mountains."

As far as I know, except for what we are told in the book of Daniel, this is also the first time the teaching about the catching away of the church has taken place in any detail. There are Old Testament texts that allude to it indirectly, but it is not spelled out or defined the way it is here. This warning has kept the expectation of His return in the forefront of our minds, and teachings about the second coming of Jesus.

But moreover, this warning to be on the alert and watching is a call to repentance for those of us who say we believe but are living in the ways of this world, asleep, living in darkness. And a call for the world to wake up. (Remember the letters of Paul to the Thessalonians.)

To Summarize

So far, I have tried to introduce the different views about the Rapture and how we know that it will happen, and then, in Matthew 24, what Jesus was allowed to tell us at that time, in accordance with the will of God the Father and what He knew at that time. But this is not all that Jesus had to say about it; He gives us more information after His resurrection in the book of Revelation, after His ascension into heaven.

THE BOOK OF REVELATIONS AND WHAT THE HOLLY SPIRIT TOLD ME IN MY SPIRIT

TODAY, WHEN WE hear someone say, "God told me," they are speaking of the Holy Spirit putting something in their spirit, not an audible voice speaking. A still, quiet voice, not an audible sound that can be heard with the ear. And that is what I am referring to here.

As I have mentioned in the introduction, God shared with me something about the texts in the book of Revelation. It has to do with Revelation 11:3 and 4 and the two witnesses. These verses are inclusive and deal with more than only the two witnesses.

So, who are the two witnesses, the two olive trees, and the two lampstands?

Revelation 11

"Then there was given me a measuring rod like a staff; and someone said, 'Get up and measure the temple of God and the altar, and those who worship in it. Leave out the court which is outside the temple and do not measure it, for it has been given to the nations; and they will tread underfoot the holy city for forty-two months. And I will grant authority to my two witnesses, and they will prophesy for twelve hundred and sixty days, clothed in sackcloth.' These are the two olive trees and the two lampstands that stand before the Lord of the earth. And if anyone wants to harm them, fire flows out of their mouth and devours their enemies; so if anyone wants to harm them, he must be killed in this way. These have the power to shut up the sky, so that rain will not fall during the days of their prophesying; and they have power over the waters to turn them into blood, and to strike the earth with every plague, as often as they desire.

When they have finished their testimony, the beast that comes up out of the abyss will make war with them, and overcome them and kill them. And their dead bodies will lie in the street of the great city which mystically is called Sodom and Egypt, where also their Lord was crucified. Those from the peoples and tribes and tongues and nations will look at their dead bodies for three and a half days, and will not permit their dead bodies to be laid in a tomb. And those who dwell on the earth will rejoice over them and celebrate; and they will send gifts to one another, because these two prophets tormented those who dwell on the earth.

But after the three and a half days, the breath of life from God came into them, and they stood on their feet; and great fear fell upon those who were watching them. And they heard a loud voice from heaven saying to them, 'Come up here.' Then they went up into heaven in the cloud, and their enemies watched them. And in that hour there was a great earthquake, and a tenth of the city fell; seven thousand people were killed in the earthquake, and the rest were terrified and gave glory to the God of heaven.

The second woe is past; behold, the third woe is coming quickly." (Verses 1–14)

> The language used in Revelation verses 11:3 and 4 is inclusive.

> "And I will grant authority to my two witnesses, and they will prophesy for twelve hundred and sixty days, clothed in sackcloth. These are the two olive trees and the two lampstands that stand before the Lord of the earth." (Revelation 11:3–4)

As I began to search out what the Bible says about the olive tree, I found verses about the olive being good for ointments and being good for the skin, or food. Or the olive leaf/branch being a symbol of peace and things along those lines. But not too much about the tree, that is until I came to Zechariah chapters 3 and 4. It is at the end of chapter 4 that brings in chapter 3.

> "Then he showed me Joshua the high priest standing before the angel of the LORD, and Satan standing at his right hand to accuse him. The LORD said to Satan, 'The LORD rebuke you, Satan! Indeed, the LORD who has chosen Jerusalem rebuke you! Is this not a brand plucked from the fire?' Now Joshua was clothed with filthy garments and standing before the angel. He spoke and said to those who were standing before him, saying, 'Remove the filthy garments from him.' Again he said to him, 'See, I have taken your iniquity away from you and will clothe you with festal robes.' Then I said, 'Let them put a clean turban on his head.' So they put a clean turban on his head and clothed him with garments, while the angel of the LORD was standing by.
>
> And the angel of the LORD admonished Joshua, saying, 'Thus says the LORD of hosts, If you will walk in My ways and if you will perform My service, then you will also govern My house and also have charge of My courts, and I will grant you free access among these who are standing here.
>
> Now listen, Joshua the high priest, you and your friends who are sitting in front of you—indeed they are men who are a symbol, for behold, I am going to bring in My servant the Branch. For behold, the stone that I have set before Joshua; on one stone are seven eyes.

Behold, I will engrave an inscription on it,' declares the LORD of hosts, 'and I will remove the iniquity of that land in one day. 10 'In that day,' declares the LORD of hosts, 'every one of you will invite his neighbor to sit under his vine and under his fig tree.'" (Zechariah 3:1–9)

"Then the angel who was speaking with me returned and roused me, as a man who is awakened from his sleep. He said to me, 'What do you see?' And I said, 'I see, and behold, a lampstand all of gold with its bowl on the top of it, and its seven lamps on it with seven spouts belonging to each of the lamps which are on the top of it; also two olive trees by it, one on the right side of the bowl and the other on its left side.' Then I said to the angel who was speaking with me saying, 'What are these, my lord?' So the angel who was speaking with me answered and said to me, 'Do you not know what these are?' And I said, 'No, my lord.' Then he said to me, 'This is the word of the LORD to Zerubbabel saying, 'Not by might nor by power, but by My Spirit,' says the LORD of hosts.' 'What are you, O great mountain? Before Zerubbabel you will become a plain; and he will bring forth the top stone with shouts of 'Grace, grace to it!'

Also the word of the LORD came to me, saying, 'The hands of Zerubbabel have laid the foundation of this house, and his hands will finish it. Then you will know that the LORD of hosts has sent me to you. For who has despised the day of small things? But these seven will be glad when they see the plumb line in the hand of Zerubbabel—these are the eyes of the LORD which range to and fro throughout the earth.'

Then I said to him, 'What are these two olive trees on the right of the lampstand and on its left?' And I answered the second time and said to him, 'What are the two olive branches which are beside the two golden pipes, which empty the golden oil from themselves?' 13 So he answered me, saying, 'Do you not know what these are?' And I said, 'No, my lord.' 14 Then he said, 'These are the two anointed ones who are standing by the Lord of the whole earth.'" (Zechariah 4:1–14)

Zechariah is told by the angel in verses 4:2–3 about the seven lampstands and two olive trees, and then in verse 4:14 that these two are the anointed ones who stand before the Lord of the whole earth. However, chapter 4 primarily speaks of Zerubbabel, which brings in chapter 3 and Joshua the high priest.

In 3:1–7, we find Joshua the high priest standing before the angel of the Lord, being accused by Satan. The angel of the Lord rebukes Satan and tells Joshua He has removed his iniquity and his filthy clothes, representing his sin.

Then in verse 8 (NKJV), Joshua is told,

"Listen, you and your friends sitting with you—indeed they are men who are a symbol..." "...for they are a wondrous sign."

We can see the prophetic intent of the text being inclusive and telescoping into the future with verses 3:8 through 10.

"'For behold, I am going to bring in My servant the Branch. For behold, the stone that I have set before Joshua; on one stone are seven eyes. Behold, I will engrave an inscription on it,' declares the LORD of hosts, 'and I will remove the iniquity of that land in one day.' 'In that day,' declares the LORD of hosts, 'every one of you will invite his neighbor to sit under his vine and under his fig tree.'"

Jesus Christ is the branch, and He removed the iniquity of the land, the world, in one day with His crucifixion. And He gave us the great commission that we are to invite everyone to come. We also see that He placed a stone before Joshua. More than one because on one there are seven eyes on it.

This brings us to chapter four, the lampstand, the olive trees, and Zerubbabel.

In verses 4:1–3, Zechariah is told of the seven lampstands and the two olive trees. Zechariah asks what these are, and in verses 6 and 7, the angel answers. But instead of explaining the trees and lampstand, He speaks of or to Zerubbabel.

> "Then the angel who was speaking with me returned and roused me, as a man who is awakened from his sleep. He said to me, 'What do you see?' And I said, 'I see, and behold, a lampstand all of gold with its bowl on the top of it, and its seven lamps on it with seven spouts belonging to each of the lamps which are on the top of it; also two olive trees by it, one on the right side of the bowl and the other on its left side.'
>
> Then he said to me, 'This is the word of the LORD to Zerubbabel saying, 'Not by might nor by power, but by My Spirit,' says the LORD of hosts. 'What are you, O great mountain? Before Zerubbabel you will become a plain; and he will bring forth the top stone with shouts of 'Grace, grace to it!'" (Zechariah 4:1–7)

In verse 6, God tells us that this person will be born again, not just being moved by God but he will know the Holy Spirit of God.

Verse 7, in my opinion, has to do with where the third temple is going to be. There is a hill near the Gihon Spring that was leveled, and there are people, scholars, who believe this is where the temple of God will be built. Maybe, maybe not.

One thing we can be sure of is that Zerubbabel did not preach grace during his life as governor. For a Jew to call someone to repent is to call them to become a Jew and live under the law of God the Father, not under the grace of Jesus. However, when we come to verses 11 through 14, the text becomes more defining. When Zechariah asks again about the two olive trees and then the two olive branches, we can understand that the branches are not the same as before. In Zechariah 3:8, the branch is Jesus; in Zechariah 4:12, the branches are branches of the trees. The two olive trees are beside two golden pipes of the lamps that pour out the golden oil from themselves. And then finally, the angel answers Zechariah, defining all of this by saying in verse 14:

> "Then he said, 'These are the two anointed ones who are standing by the Lord of the whole earth.'"

It is this verse, given to us by God the Father, that ties Zechariah chapters 3 and 4 to the two witnesses of Revelation 11:

> "And I will grant authority to my two witnesses, and they will prophesy for twelve hundred and sixty days, clothed in sackcloth. These are the two olive trees and the two lampstands that stand before the Lord of the earth." (Revelation 11:3–4)

Revelation 1:20 explains further,

> "And the seven lampstands are the seven churches."

> "And I will grant authority to my two witnesses, and they will prophesy for twelve hundred and

sixty days, clothed in sackcloth." (Revelation 11:3)

We know that Jesus tells us in the book of Revelation in the letters to the seven churches that they are the seven lamps that stand before the Lord.

> "When I saw Him, I fell at His feet like a dead man. And He placed His right hand on me, saying, 'Do not be afraid; I am the first and the last, and the living One; and I was dead, and behold, I am alive forevermore, and I have the keys of death and of Hades. Therefore write the things which you have seen, and the things which are, and the things which will take place after these things. As for the mystery of the seven stars which you saw in My right hand, and the seven golden lampstands: the seven stars are the angels of the seven churches, and the seven lampstands are the seven churches.'" (Revelation 1:17–20)

Okay, in Zechariah 4, we have the olive trees and the lampstands. And then in Revelation 1:20, Jesus defines the seven lampstands. But there is another defining moment in Zechariah 4, given by the angel speaking with Zechariah.

> "Then I said to him, 'What are these two olive trees on the right of the lampstand and on its left?' And I answered the second time and said to him, 'What are the two olive branches which are beside the two golden pipes, which empty the golden oil from themselves?' So he answered me, saying, 'Do you not know what these are?' And I said, 'No, my lord.' Then he said, 'These are the two anointed ones who are standing by the Lord of the whole earth.'" (Zechariah 4:11–14)

Joshua the high priest and Zerubbabel are the two anointed witnesses that stand before the Lord of the earth.

Revelations
Message to Smyrna

"And to the angel of the church in Smyrna write: The first and the last, who was dead, and has come to life, says this: 'I know your tribulation and your poverty (but you are rich), and the blasphemy by those who say they are Jews and are not, but are a synagogue of Satan. Do not fear what you are about to suffer. Behold, the devil is about to cast some of you into prison, so that you will be tested, and you will have tribulation for ten days. Be faithful until death, and I will give you the crown of life. He who has an ear, let him hear what the Spirit says to the churches. He who overcomes will not be hurt by the second death.'"
(Revelation 2:8–11)

Jesus does not hold anything against the church of Smyrna.
Message to Philadelphia:

"And to the angel of the church in Philadelphia write: He who is holy, who is true, who has the key of David, who opens and no one will shut, and who shuts and no one opens, says this: 'I know your deeds. Behold, I have put before you an open door which no one can shut, because you have a little power, and have kept My word, and have not denied My name. Behold, I will cause those of the synagogue of Satan, who say that they are Jews and are not, but lie—I will make them come and bow down at your feet, and make them know that I have loved you. Because you have kept the word of My perseverance, I also will keep you from the hour of testing, that hour which is about to come upon the whole world, to test those who dwell on the earth. I am coming quickly; hold fast what you have, so that no one will take your crown. He who overcomes, I will make him a pillar in the temple of My God, and he will not go out from it anymore; and I will write on him the name of My God, and the name of the city of My God, the new Jerusalem, which comes down out of heaven from My God, and My new name. He who has an ear, let him hear what the Spirit says to the churches.'" (Revelation 3:7–13)

The church of Philadelphia has nothing held against it and is also promised to be kept from the hour of testing, the great tribulation. These two churches are the two lampstands the two witnesses represent. And we can see that the two olive trees are the faithful Jewish people of God if we consider Joshua the son of Nun, and Caleb of the twelve spies that entered the promised land.

Daniel and the End Time

"Now at that time Michael, the great prince who stands guard over the sons of your people, will arise. And there will be a time of distress such as never occurred since there was a nation until that time; and at that time your people, everyone who is found written in the book, will be rescued. Many of those who sleep in the dust of the ground will awake, these to everlasting life, but the others to disgrace and everlasting contempt. Those who have insight will shine brightly like the brightness of the expanse of heaven, and those who lead the many to righteousness, like the stars forever and ever. But as for you, Daniel, conceal these words and seal up the book until the end of time; many will go back and forth, and knowledge will increase.

Then I, Daniel, looked and behold, two others were standing, one on this bank of the river and the other on that bank of the river. And one said to the man dressed in linen, who was above the waters of the river, 'How long will it be until the end of these wonders?' I heard the man dressed in linen, who was above the waters of the river, as he raised his right hand and his left toward heaven, and swore by Him who lives forever that it would be for a time, times, and half a time; and as soon as they finish shattering the power of the holy people, all these events will be completed. As for me, I heard but could not understand; so I said, 'My lord, what will be the outcome of these events?' He said, 'Go your way, Daniel, for these words are concealed and sealed up until the end time. Many will be purged, purified, and refined, but the wicked will act wickedly; and none of the wicked will understand, but those who have insight will understand. From the time that the regular sacrifice is abolished and the abomination of desolation is set up, there will be 1,290 days. How blessed is he who keeps waiting and attains to the 1,335 days! But as for you, go your way to the end; then you will enter into rest and rise again for your allotted portion at the end of the age.'" (Daniel 12:1–12)

These texts are from Daniel's seventieth week, the seven years of tribulation.

When Michael, the archangel, stands, it is the halfway point and the beginning of great tribulation. "Distress such as never occurred."

At that time, God's people found written in the Book of Life will be rescued. Those who are asleep in the dust and written in the book will awake and be resurrected, and we who remain will be caught up with them. The two people standing on opposite sides of the river are most likely the two witnesses, each coming from different countries. I can't help but consider that Isaiah 28 has to do with one of the witnesses.

> "Indeed, He will speak to this people through
> stammering lips and a foreign tongue, He who
> said to them, 'Here is rest, give rest to the weary,'
> and, 'Here is repose,' but they would not listen."
> (Isaiah 28:11–12)

Then one of the two men asks someone above the water of the river how long to the end of these wonders, those being rescued and those that sleep in the dust awake. And he answers, saying "It will be time, times, and half a time," which is the same amount of time as the testimony of the two witnesses when they have shattered the power of God's people, that being the stopping of the animal sacrifice and the abomination of desolation by the antichrist.

Then Daniel is told,

> "But as for you, go your way to the end; then you
> will enter into rest and rise again for your allotted
> portion at the end of the age." (Isaiah 28:13)

Daniel will be raised with those who sleep in the dust into rest, God's rest, and receive his reward.

The Links

> "And the seven lampstands are the seven churches."
> (Revelation 1:20)

> "And I will grant authority to my two witnesses, and they will prophesy for twelve hundred and sixty days, clothed in sackcloth." (Revelation 11:3)

> "These are the two olive trees and the two lampstands that stand before the Lord of the earth." (Revelation 11:4)

> "Then I said to him, 'What are these two olive trees on the right of the lampstand and on its left?'" (Zechariah 4:11)

> "And I answered the second time and said to him, 'What are the two olive branches which are beside the two golden pipes, which empty the golden oil from themselves?'" (Zechariah 4:12)

> "Then he said, 'These are the two anointed ones who are standing by the Lord of the whole earth.'" (Zechariah 4:14)

The angel tells us that the two olive trees and the two lampstands are the two anointed ones that stand before the Lord. But chapter 4 only speaks of Zerubbabel, which brings in chapter 3 and Joshua the high priest.

> "Now listen, Joshua the high priest, you and your friends who are sitting in front of you—indeed they are men who are a symbol." (Zechariah 3:8)

> "Hear, O Joshua, the high priest, you and your companions who sit before you, for they are a wondrous sign." (Zechariah 3:8 NKJV)

While I am not a professional writer or a biblical scholar, I have made my best effort to present what God has shown me in His written Word, the Bible. I know traditionalists and people with strong opinions or beliefs about what they have been taught will disagree, but I believe this work to be correct. It is conclusive, ties everything together, and makes no assumptions. Furthermore, it fits the known history of the Bible and the character of God.

> "The only barrier to truth is the presumption that you already have it." (Chuck Missler)

I grew up being taught the pre-tribulation Rapture, and that it would be sudden and unannounced. But after studying and hearing other views, I concluded that these teachings make God a liar.

> "Surely the Lord God does nothing unless He reveals His secret counsel to His servants the prophets." (Amos 3:7)

God is going to raise up His two witnesses. I believe they will be Jewish. They will have the spirits of Joshua the high priest and Zerubbabel. They will testify to the Jewish community in Israel the name of Jesus Christ and His grace until they are martyred. Jesus will descend from heaven in the clouds, but He will not touch the ground.

Jesus will breathe the breath of life into His two witnesses (two branches) and call them to "come up here." They will be caught up to Him along with the two olive trees, the faithful Jewish people of the Old Testament days. Along with the two lamps that pour out the golden oil, the Spirit, represented by the churches of Philadelphia and Smyrna, those true Christians found without blame.

Then those who are alive and remain will be caught up together with them to be in the presence of God, and the protective hand of God will be lifted.

This is going to take place, not in secret, but before the entire earth. Everyone will see. All the world will know, and the mystery of God will be finished.

It will be this knowledge that carries the weight of the mark of the Antichrist.

All those who are left behind in this world will make a conscious decision, fully aware of the choice being made.

Do you want to live in this world free to do whatever you want regardless of the harm it causes to you or others, and death being the consequence? Or will you choose life in a world where there is no more death or rape, and murder will be ended, no more child abuse or incest? The world to come is a world where everyone will live with love, not only for yourself but for others as well. If you are not a person who has believed in Jesus, or you haven't been living by your faith, now is the time to change. Now is the time Jesus is knocking at the door and the day of grace.

A prayer of confession:

Lord Jesus, I know I am a sinner, doing things that cause harm to myself or others. Forgive me for the things I do that I know are wrong, and come into my life and into my heart. Deliver me into Your grace and mercy. Keep me for Your namesake now and forever. In the name of Jesus, I pray and ask these things to the glory of God. Amen.

ABOUT THE AUTHOR

THERE IS NOTHING remarkable about me; I am a blue-collar type of person (a truck driver). However, I do like to study the Bible.

In 2010, I was conducting an in-depth study of the Rapture. At that time, my wife and I were attending a group Bible study that caused me to explore other subject-based studies, from angels and fallen angels to Christophanies, among others.

Then in 2016, my wife and I suffered the tragic loss of one of our adult children. Afterward, with few exceptions, I could not study the Bible. Until around November 2022, God instilled in my spirit something about the language used in the prophecies of the book of Revelation. This is the resulting work.

www.ingramcontent.com/pod-product-compliance
Lightning Source LLC
Chambersburg PA
CBHW021150130726
47988CB00004B/1539

9798893454550